Orangutans

By Christy Steele

Steadwell Books

Raintree Steck-Vaughn Publishers

A Harcourt Company

Austin · New York

www.steck-vaughn.com

ANIMALS OF THE RAIN FOREST

Published by Raintree Steck-Vaughn Publishers,
an imprint of Steck-Vaughn Company.

Library of Congress Cataloging-in-Publication Data
Cataloging-in-Publication data is available upon request.

Produced by Compass Books

Photo Acknowledgments
Digital Stock, cover; Photophile/Roger Holden, 8, 16, 19, 23, 24
Root Resources/Anthony Mercieca, 4-5
Visuals Unlimited, Kjell B. Sandved, title page, 15; C.R. George, 11, 20;
 Gary W. Carter, 12; Inga Spence, 27, 28

Content Consultants   *3306246*
Cheryl Knott, Ph.D.
Orangutan Project International
Assistant Professor of Anthropology
Harvard University

Maria Kent Rowell
Science Consultant
Sebastopol, California

David Larwa
National Science Education Consultant
Educational Training Services
Brighton, Michigan

Contents

MALAYSIA

South China Sea

MALAYSIA

BORNEO

SUMATRA

Java Sea

JAVA

Range of the Orangutan

Surrounding Land

Water

Borders

N
W E
S

A Quick Look at Orangutans

What do orangutans look like?
Orangutans are large, hairy, red-brown apes. They have long hands, arms, and feet.

Where do orangutans live?
Orangutans live in rain forests on the islands of Borneo and Sumatra in southeast Asia.

What do orangutans eat?
Orangutans eat mostly fruit. They also eat leaves, bark, and insects when they cannot find enough fruit to eat.

How many orangutans are there?
Only about 25,000 orangutans live in the wild. They are in danger of dying out.

Orangutans are the largest apes living in Asia.

Orangutans in Rain Forests

Orangutans are mammals. A mammal is a warm-blooded animal with a backbone. Warm-blooded animals have a body temperature that stays the same even when it is hot or cold outside. Temperature is a measure of heat or cold.

Orangutans are important to life in the rain forest. Rain forests are places where many trees and plants grow close together and much rain falls. Orangutans eat many kinds of fruit. Some seeds from the fruit leave their bodies in the form of waste. Waste is what a body does not use or need of food that has been eaten. Some new plants grow from these seeds and the plants spread.

Smart Animals

Scientists have learned that orangutans are some of the smartest animals. Scientists have taught them to point to shapes or use **sign language** to talk. Sign language is a way of using hand movements to stand for words.

Orangutans make and use simple tools. Wild orangutans use sticks to get seeds out of some fruit. They also put sticks into holes and wait for insects to climb on. They pull the sticks out and eat the insects.

Where Orangutans Live

There are two places in southeast Asia where orangutans live. One place is the island of Sumatra. Sumatra belongs to the country of Indonesia. The other place orangutans live is on the island of Borneo. Part of Borneo belongs to Indonesia, too. The other part of Borneo belongs to the country of Malaysia.

Most orangutans live near rivers in warm lowland **habitats**. A habitat is a place where an animal or plant usually lives.

Orangutans live in the trees of the rain forest.

▲ This male orangutan has large cheek pads and long, red-brown hair.

Canopy

Orangutans live mostly in the trees of the rain forest. This area of thick leaves and branches is called the forest **canopy**.

The canopy has lower, middle, and upper parts. Orangutans live in the lower and middle canopy, from 20 feet (6 m) to 100 feet

(30 m) above the ground. The upper canopy is about 150 feet (46 m) above the ground.

What Orangutans Look Like

Orangutans are large apes. Males can grow up to 5 feet (1.5 m) tall. They may weigh up to 220 pounds (100 kg). Females are smaller. They usually weigh up to 120 pounds (54 kg).

The orangutan's coloring is different from other kinds of apes. Long, red-brown hair covers their bodies. Most other apes have black hair.

Fully grown male orangutans have large pads growing from their cheeks. They have a **sac** hanging from their necks. A sac is part of an animal or plant that is shaped like a bag.

Male orangutans make a special sound so other males know where they are. Scientists call the sound a **long call**. It sounds like a roar. To make the long call, the male breathes deeply. When he breathes out, the air makes the loud sound.

Life in Trees

An orangutan's body is good for traveling in trees. Orangutans have long, strong arms. Their arms are longer than their legs. Orangutans' hands and feet are long and thin. They have moveable thumbs on their hands. Their fingers and toes can bend and curl around branches.

Orangutans are always moving around the rain forest canopy. They have home ranges. A home range is the space where an animal lives out most of its life. Orangutans live and find food in their home ranges. Females have smaller home ranges than males.

Orangutans move through the canopy using all four hands and feet at the same time. Three of the four are usually holding onto something. They pull themselves along like people do when climbing. This way of moving through trees is called **slow clambering**.

If there is a lot of space between trees, orangutans shake the trees they are on back

▲ **This young orangutan is using both its hands and feet to move through the trees.**

and forth. They do this until they can grab the next tree over and climb on.

Every night, orangutans bend over small tree branches to build nests to sleep in. They build them anywhere from 30 to 85 feet (9.2 to 25.9 m) above the ground.

Orangutans eat leaves from plants when they cannot find fruit.

Food

Orangutans spend a great deal of time looking for food. They spend 60% to 70% of their day finding, picking, and eating fruit, bark, leaves, and insects.

Sometimes there is more fruit to be found in the rain forests where orangutans live. This happens because of **mast fruiting**. Mast fruiting is when most of the fruit trees all grow fruit at the same time. This happens about every three to seven years. Food is easy for orangutans to find at this time.

After mast fruiting, there are often many months with little fruit growth. Food is harder for orangutans to find during these months.

Kinds of Food

Scientists have learned that orangutans eat about 400 different kinds of food. They eat plants most of the time, but will sometimes eat insects.

Orangutans eat mainly fruits and nuts. They eat a lot of durians. A durian is a large, round, green fruit with soft, sweet-tasting insides. They smell bad and have very long spikes.

Sometimes there is not much fruit in the rain forests. Orangutans must then find bark, leaves, and insects to eat.

Orangutans eat so much fruit during mast fruiting that they gain weight. This extra weight is fat. Their bodies turn the fat into energy when there is not much fruit.

 An orangutan at the Metrozoo in Miami, Florida, stopped eating. A zookeeper created a special cake made of apples, oranges, bananas, carrots, squash, eggs, monkey biscuits, and oatmeal. The orangutan liked the cake so much that it began eating again.

Orangutans spend most of their time finding and eating food.

Young orangutans travel around the rain forest with their mothers.

An Orangutan's Life Cycle

Orangutans do not live together in large groups. Males live alone because they do not get along with other males. Mother orangutans often live with one or two of their young. Sometimes young female orangutans of the same age travel together.

Orangutans come together most during mast fruiting. They also mate most often during mast fruiting. Females have more energy to mate then.

Scientists are not sure how long wild orangutans live. They think that wild orangutans live anywhere from 30 to 45 years. They know that orangutans in zoos can live up to 50 years.

Mating

Male orangutans are ready to mate when they are about 15 years old. Then they can mate whenever they find females that are willing to mate with them. Often, females will not mate with a male until his cheek pads are fully grown. This does not happen until the males are about 20 years old.

Female orangutans are ready to mate when they are about 12 years old. The females mate once about every seven or eight years.

Young

Female orangutans give birth eight and one-half months after mating. At birth, orangutans weigh about 4 pounds (2 kg). They drink their mother's milk. For the first few years, young orangutans ride on their mothers while learning how to move about on their own.

Young orangutans live with their mothers. Young orangutans learn how to find and eat

▲ **Mother orangutans find food and feed it to their young.**

fruit, leaves, bark, and insects. They learn how to make nests.

Orangutans leave their mothers when they are 10 to 12 years old. Females stay close to their mothers' home ranges. Males often travel far away.

In the Malay language, orangutan means person of the forest.

Living with Orangutans

Scientists believe orangutans are a lot like humans. They study orangutans to find out what early human ancestors might have been like. An ancestor is a family member who lived a long time ago.

Orangutans are **endangered**. Endangered means all the orangutans could die out if things are not done to protect them and their habitats. Scientists believe there are only about 25,000 orangutans left in the wild.

Orangutans in Danger

Orangutans are losing their habitat. Huge fires have burned many miles of the rain forest. In 1997, forest fires killed about 1,000 orangutans. People are also cutting down many trees in the rain forest. Some want to build homes and plant crops there. Some want to sell the wood.

Hunting also kills many orangutans. In Indonesia and Malaysia, it is against the law to hunt, sell, or keep pet orangutans. Many people break the law to make money. Hunters kill mother orangutans and take their young. They sell the young to people who want them for pets.

Over time, orangutans grow too large and owners cannot take care of them. These orangutans cannot go back to the wild. Their mothers never taught them how to live in the rain forest.

Many orangutans are friendly to people. This is why people want pet orangutans. Still, orangutans should not be taken from their homes in the rain forest.

These orangutans live in a protected wildlife station.

Saving Orangutans

Some people are trying to save orangutans. They have built stations and centers to help them.

At the stations, scientists study wild orangutans. This helps save the rain forest where the stations are located. This is one of the best ways to save parts of the rain forest.

At the centers, workers take care of sick or hurt orangutans. They also raise young orangutans whose mothers have died. They teach these animals to live in the wild. People hope these actions will help stop orangutans from dying out.

Glossary

canopy (KAN-uh-pee)—a thick area of leaves high up in the treetops

endangered (en-DAYN-jurd)—in danger of dying out

habitat (HAB-i-tat)—the place where an animal or plant usually lives

long call (LONG KAWL)—a sound like a roar that male orangutans make

mast fruiting (MAST FROOT-ing)—a time during which most fruit trees grow fruit all at the same time

sac (SAK)—an animal or plant part that is shaped like a bag

sign language (SINE LANG-gwij)—a language in which hand movements are used instead of speech

slow clambering (SLOH KLAM-bur-ing)—a way of moving through trees using both hands and both feet

Internet Sites

The Balikpapan Orangutan Society
http://www.orangutan.com

Orangutan Foundation International
http://www.orangutan.org

Sumatran Orangutan Society
http://www.cavespider.com/orangutan/

Useful Addresses

The Gunung Palung Orangutan Project
Harvard University
Department of Anthropology
11 Divinity Avenue
Cambridge, MA 02138

Orangutan Foundation International
822 South Wellesley Avenue
Los Angeles, CA 90049

Index